A BEE NAME
AND OTHER POEMS

by Candace A. Dietz
Illustrations by Virginia J. Rost

Published by

MIXED MEDIA
MEMOIRS

Mixed Media Memoirs LLC
2802 W. Carrera Court
Green Bay, WI 54311
mixedmediamemoirs@new.rr.com

Cover and Book design by Laura Treichel

A Bee Named Bea and Other Poems

Manufactured in the United States of America

For my grandchildren:
Arin, William, Connor, Grace, Patrick,
Quinn, Lionel & Kempie.

– C. D.

For my grandchildren James, Augie, and newborn Virginia Kathleen.
And for those to come.

– V. R.

AN ALLIGATOR NAMED AUGIE

An alligator named Augie
Went out to the bog
When it was quite foggy
To find his friend, Froggy.

"Oh, Froggy, where are you?"
Yelled alligator Augie,
"I can't see so well
Because it's too smoggy."

"Here I am, Augie,
Over here," said Froggy.
"Please, oh please,
Don't bite me, Augie!"

"Why, Froggy, I'm just a baby gator.
All I do is smile and coo.
Of course I won't bite you!"

So Augie and Froggy, a trifle soggy,
Sat on a log in the foggy, smoggy bog
Chanting: "Coo, Ribbit, Coo, Ribbit,
Coo, Ribbit, Coo."

A BEE NAMED BEA

A bee named Bea
Said, "Mercy me—
Everyone's afraid of me!

When I try to be a friendly bee
They zoom away and let me be—

Just me, Bea, by myself.

One day I flew into a flower.
Two girls in the grass cried
'Eek a Bee!' They ran away
And left me to play—

Just me, Bea, by myself.

Then I flew into a garden.
Wee, lucky me! What a lovely treat—
So much nectar for me to eat!

'Oh, no!' said a lady, sipping tea.
She took her cup and let me be—

Just me, Bea, by myself.

Lonely, lonely, lonely me.
Just me, a lonely, lonely bee.

That afternoon I heard a buzz—
A bug with black and yellow fuzz!
Mercy me—a bee like me!
Won't you come and play with me?

Now I buzz around with glee.
Merry Bee will play with me!
And we're as happy as can be—
Merry Bee and me, just Bea.

Buzzzzzzzzzzzz. Buzzzzzzzzzzzz."

A BIRD
NAMED DICKIE

A bird named Dickie
Was very, very tricky.
He wanted all the food at the feeder.
He shoved the other birds away.
Oh, he was *quite* the leader.

"Me first, me first," said Dickie.
"I'm very, very hungry."
"You wait. I'm stuck," said Dickie,
"These seeds are very sticky!"

The other birds just had to wait.
They were afraid of Dickie.
And by the time they got their turn,
The few seeds left were icky!

"You need to share—it's only fair,"
The other birds told Dickie.
"Okay, I'll mosey over there
So you can eat," sighed Dickie.

"You first, you first," moaned Dickie,
He was no longer tricky.
"You first, you first," groaned Dickie,
"My tummy's feeling sicky!"

A BUNNY NAMED PAUL

A bunny named Paul came to play
In my grandpa's garage for the day.
His Mama appeared at night to say:

"Paul, come out! Don't dawdle at all!
A garage is no place for a bunny named Paul.
Not at all. No, not at all!"

Paul looked at his mother
    and said:
"But I like it here inside
    this stall
It's warm in here—not cold
    at all."

"Paul, come out. It's time for bed.
Come right now!" his Mama said.
"Your brother and sister went ahead."

"Please, Mama Bunny, can I stay the night?
There's nothing here to give you fright.
I like this Jeep. It's really neat.
And the man who drives it is kind and sweet.
He gave me a carrot for a treat,
A midnight snack I hope to eat."

"Paul, I don't like this at all!
You're still too small
To stay alone in a stall."

So Paul, who was a good bunny, said:
"Okay, Mama, you know best.
I know I need my bunny rest.
I'll come with you to our bunny nest."

Remember, baby bunnies:
Mama bunny knows best.
Sleep tight, one and all
Like the bunny named Paul.

A BUTTERFLY NAMED ARIN

A butterfly named Arin—
That's Arin with an "A"—
Fluttered and flitted, floated
        and flew
Around the yard all day.

"Arin," said her mother,
"Can't you please sit still?"
And Arin, happy Arin, said,
"Oh, sure, of course I will!"

She tried to keep her wings still
And nap for a few minutes.
But trying to be quiet—
There just was no fun in it.

Though she was really trying,
Arin started to giggle
When one wing then the other wing
Began to twitch and wiggle!

She laughed aloud and fluttered around,
Then tried to be still again.
"Oh my, oh dear," said Arin,
I cannot seem to win!
I just have so much energy
That sitting still won't work for me!"

So her wise and wonderful mother said,
"I know just what to do.
We'll sign you up for gymnastics.
It's perfect for someone like you!"

And Arin, happy Arin
Was even happier still.
"Will I do gymnastics?
You bet your wings I will!"

So Arin joined gymnastics class
And flopped and fluttered and flew
And high-vaulted and back-flipped
And cartwheeled loop-di-loo.

That afternoon at rest time—
It's hard to believe but true—
Arin was still and quiet.
And she took a long nap, too.

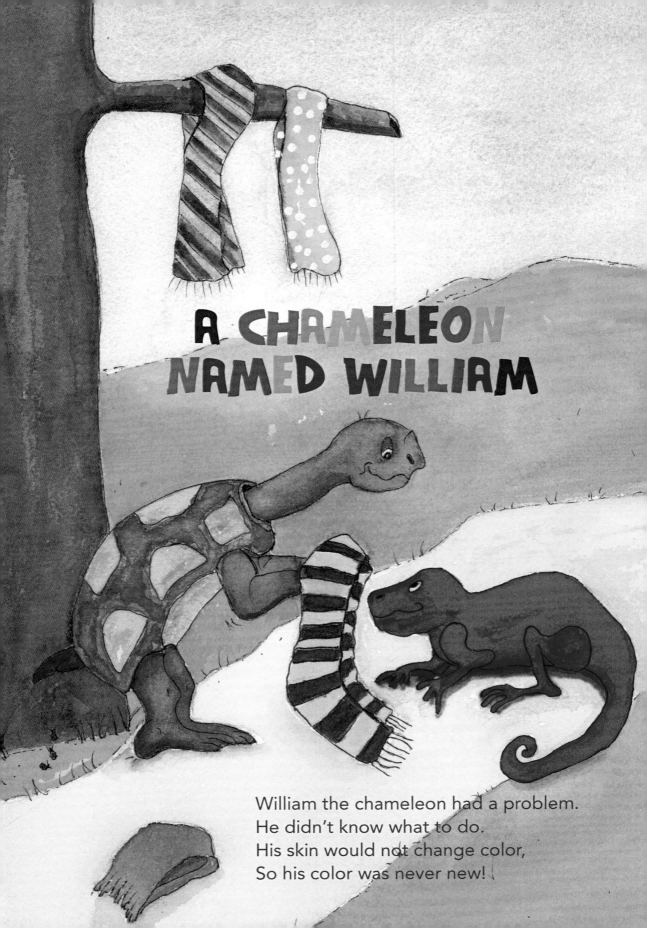

A CHAMELEON NAMED WILLIAM

William the chameleon had a problem.
He didn't know what to do.
His skin would not change color,
So his color was never new!

William the vermilion chameleon
Never could be blue
Or yellow or orange or green
Or pink or brown in hue.

Other chameleons could change
Into any shade that thrilled them.
But William the vermilion chameleon
Always stayed vermilion.

He cried "What to do? What to do? What to do?"
"Well, William," said his friend Turtle,
"I have an idea for you.
What if you wear a colorful scarf—
For something different and new?"

Then Turtle pulled from his shell
Scarves of every color—and scarves
With multicolored stars,
Polka dots, stripes, triangles and bars!

Now William can change from vermilion
Into the colors that thrill him—
Yellow or green or purple or blue.
But some days he just stays vermilion.
Because that's a great color, too.

A canary named Larry couldn't be merry
Because he couldn't sing.

Whenever he squeaked a song out
The other birds' ears would ring.

"Larry, Larry, please don't sing!"
Begged the other canaries.
"You're all off-key. Your dongs—they ding!
Your singing makes our poor ears ring."

Poor Larry, poor Larry,
The off-key canary.
He really couldn't sing.
Then Larry, bright Larry,
The clever canary,
Chirped "I'll try a *new* thing.

A bell! A bell! It's just as well—
I'll ring a bell instead.
A bell is crisp and clear and bright.
Its song won't hurt your head!"

So Larry rang a little bell
That had a tuneful, pleasing knell.
The other canaries sang and sang
And Larry rang his bell.

And Larry was finally merry
Because he could ring so well.

A CHICKEN NAMED CHARLIE

A chicken named Charlie rode a little Harley
Around the barnyard one day.
He became a little careless—
And even a bit scareless—
And decided to go wings away.

"Wings away, wings away," yelled Charlie,
As he lifted his wings from the bars.
"Wings away! Wings away! Hip hip hooray!"
And then he rolled right into the hay.

"Charlie, Charlie," said his best friend Marley,
"You need both wings on the bars!
Charlie, if you don't listen to me,
Next time you'll see stars!"

So Charlie rode his Harley
Around the barnyard at noon
And kept both wings on the bars—
But he got thirsty soon!

"Wings away, wings away," yelled Charlie,
As he sipped his lemonade.
"Wings away, wings away," cried Charlie
And he rolled right into the hay.

"Charlie, Charlie," said his best friend Marley,
"You need both wings on the bars!
Charlie, if you don't listen to me,
You'll fly right off to Mars!"

So, Charlie rode his Harley.
He whistled and he sang
But kept both wings on the bars—
Until his cell phone rang.

"Wings away, wings away!" waved Charlie,
As he talked to his buddy, Clay.
"Wings away, wings away," yelled Charlie,
And he rolled right into the hay.

"Charlie, Charlie," asked his best friend Marley.
"Why are you acting this way?"
"Charlie, Charlie," inquired Marley,
"Is this a naughty Charlie day?"

"Yes," answered Charlie, picking up his Harley.
"I'm sorry I acted that way."
"And look!" said Charlie, "I've broken my Harley
By ignoring the rules for safe play!"

A COW NAMED SUE

A cow named Sue,
She liked to moo
And so she mooed loudly all the day through.
She mooed and mooed and mooed and mooed.

"Now Sue," said her Dad,
"Being quiet's not bad!
It's not always a good time to moo."
"Oh, foo," sighed Sue, "I like to moo."
"Then go to the barn," said Dad to Sue.

And so she loudly mooed and mooed and mooed
And mooed and mooed and mooed.
But after a few hours, her moo was new.
It was a soft and quiet moo.

"Oh, dear" whispered Sue,
"What happened to my moo?
I don't think I sound right. Do you?"

Her dad said, "Sue, I think you do.
You're a softer, nicer-sounding Sue.
Sometimes it's fine to be quiet, too."

Now Sue has a quieter moo.
She can moo softly.
Can you?

A CRAB NAMED CONNOR

A crab named Connor, on my honor,
Is the tiniest crab I know.

He crawls to the top of the rocks in his cage,
And then crawls down below.

He has just one pace when he moves
And it is always S L O W.

He wears a tiny little shell
And hasn't changed it yet.

He loves his tiny little shell
Connor, the crab, my pet.

He shuffles through his sand and plants
And when I take him out

He shimmies down my shirtsleeve
And tickles me crawling about.

He has one question, one burning question,
"When, oh when, will I grow?

Can you tell me? Please tell me,"
Begs Connor. "I really want to know!"

"Connor," I tell him, "Little Connor,
When you're ready, you'll grow quite well.

Your legs and claws will get bigger,
And then you'll change your shell."

Connor the crab is my tiny pet.
And he's my friend as well.

A DEER NAMED STAN

Stan the deer,
He had a sneer
He used when he was mad.

The sneer upset his dear old Dad:
"Stan, what do you sneer for
When there's so much to cheer for—
So much to make you glad?"

Stan would sneer when a car was near.
And he sneered at his playmates, too.
His friends were put off by his grouchy stare
And wouldn't play—would you?

"Happy face, Stan!
Wear a happy face, Stan!"
Said Stan's well-meaning Dad,
"Happy face, Stan!
You always look mad
Even though you should be glad!"

Stan had a habit
Of sneering at lights.
He sneered all day
and he sneered all night.

He sneered at his food.
He sneered at his bed.
He sneered at everything
Anyone said.

He sneered when he was happy.
He sneered when he was sad.
He sneered when things were good.
And he sneered when things were bad.

"Happy face, Stan!
Wear a happy face, Stan!"
Said Stan's frustrated Dad,
"Happy face, Stan!
You always look mad
Even though you should be glad!"

Then one day Stan thought he'd try something new.
He thought and thought about what to do.
He tried to turn his sneer around.
He sneered and sneered into a frown.
And then he turned it upside-down.

He turned his frown into a smile!
Stan hadn't smiled in a long, long while.

"Happy face, Stan!
That's a happy face, Stan!"
Said Stan's elated Dad,
"Happy face, Stan!
You used to look mad
And now you look so glad!"

"I'm glad," said his Dad.
"I'm glad, too, Dad," said Stan the sneering deer,
As he grinned from ear to ear.

A DOLPHIN NAMED QUINN

A dolphin named Quinn went for a swim
In the California ocean.
He had his own way to move his fins—
In fancy figure-eight motions.

He'd figure-eight around the ships
And look for interesting people.
And then he'd do a little flip
As he swam by the peep hole.

A little boy was looking out
And saw the dolphin swimming about.
The little boy called, "Dolphin, Dolphin,
Do you want to come in?"

"I can't," said Quinn, "I must stay in
The wet and salty ocean.
But we can play a game, I bet.
I'll swim some numbers for you to guess!"

So Quinn swam his favorite number, eight,
and when the boy guessed it, Quinn said, "Great!"
He swam again. The boy guessed six.
"Right! And here's another trick."

Then Quinn swam the number three:
"Can you add the numbers up for me?"
"Eight plus six plus three," said the boy
"That's seventeen!" he shouted with joy.

Dolphin Quinn said, "Good for you!
And now I've got more exploring to do."
Then Quinn the Dolphin swam away,
Figure-eighting through the bay.

Now whenever the boy looks out
On the California ocean,
He searches for Quinn, his dolphin friend,
The swimming mathematician.

A DUCK NAMED DAN

A duck named Dan
Went out to get a tan
By the waters of Green Bay.

He basked in the sunshine
And had some quiet fun time.
He was resting when he heard: "Hey, hey,

Dan! That's quite a tan!
How long have you been in the sun?
You look all red from your toes to your head.
Surely, you are done!"

"Oh," said Dan, "I wanted a tan
So I've been here all day.
I've had some quiet fun time
Resting in the sunshine,
Taking a break from play."

"Dan, my man, that's enough of a tan!
Do you really think it's O.K.
To lie around without a plan
Just soaking up sun all day?"

"Maybe not!" said Dan,
As he jumped into the bay
And quickly splashed away.

The next time Dan went
out to get a tan
By the waters of
Green Bay,
He took his watch, his
sunscreen and a hat,
Bottled water, some
crackers and a new
straw mat
And Dan didn't burn
that day!

A GIRAFFE NAMED JAMES

James, James, the dancing giraffe
Dances just to make us laugh!
He dances to the radio,
To TV, CDs and MP3s,
James, the dancing giraffe.

James has rhythm.
James has style.
James will dance and all the while
James will wear a winning smile.

At weddings and parties—
It's hard to explain—
James just has to entertain!
He'll spin off the floor
And we'll call out for more
From the dancing giraffe we all adore,
James, the dancing giraffe.

So if you're ever feeling blue
Just have James come and dance for you!
James, the affable, lovable,
Wonderfully huggable,
Giggling, dancing giraffe.

A GOOSE NAMED GRACE

A goose named Grace,
Had a pretty face
And she smiled and smiled all day.
She always shared her goosey toys.
She was darling in every way.

"You have this doll,
I'll have that one,"
She would often say.
"If I share my toys with you,
Then both of us can play!"

But then one day a new toy came,
A shiny bright pink buggy.
"I will never share this toy,"
Said Grace the goose quite smugly.

"It's so special, bouncy and pink,
I just can't let it go.
Please try hard to understand.
It's just that I love it so."

Grace's mother thought and thought
About just what to do:
"It's O.K. to have one thing
That is just for you,
When your friends come over to play,
We'll just put the buggy away!"

Grace still shared her goosey toys
But not her special buggy.
She always played with that alone
Because it was so lovely.

And then when Grace was no longer three
Something magic came to be:
One day she shared her buggy.
Can you share all of your toys, too?
Or do you have one thing just for you?

A LION CUB NAMED LIONEL

A lion cub named Lionel
Said, "Mama, this is final:
I cannot eat my peas,
So please don't feed me these.

I'll eat beans, broccoli and tomatoes,
Celery, eggplant and potatoes;
Cauliflower and carrots I'll gladly finish
And fennel, lettuce, okra, spinach.
I'll eat up linguini and all my zucchini
But please don't feed me peas.
Please, oh please, not these!

I'll eat apples, bananas, kiwi, craisins
Papaya, mango, melon, raisins,
Berries—black and red and blue—
And peaches, pears and oranges, too.
But please don't feed me these.
Please, pretty please, no peas!

I'll eat yogurt, hotdogs, turkey, too;
Ham, fish, sausage and tofu;
Eggs and liver, pizza, steak
And lots and lots of birthday cake!
But, mother, no more peas, please,
I don't want any peas."

His mother said, "You'll like *these* peas—
They're fresh from the pod. Just try them. Please."

Lionel tried the fresh baby peas.
Then he smiled and said: "Some more peas, please!"

A PENGUIN NAMED PATRICK

A penguin named Patrick
Was famous for his hat tricks
In the frozen, frozen Arctic.

He'd say "Good day to you,"
And he'd tip his hat, too,
That polite, polite young Patrick.

As he slid to school
He'd shout "Late isn't cool!"
And balance his hat on his book.

Once inside he'd spin his hat
And give the brim a little pat
Then hang it on a hook.

"No hats in school—
Yes, that's the rule,"
Said the proper, proper teacher.

On the playground
The kids would gather around
To see a new trick of Patrick's.

"Come on, Patrick,
Come on, Patrick,
Show us another hat trick!"

Patrick would bow and make a swoop
And Patrick's hat would make two loops
Before landing back on his head.

He'd do three flips
And the hat would stick—
Then he'd toss it into the breeze.
His friends would call, "More tricks,
More tricks, Patrick, please!"

But at the bell Patrick would call it a day,
He'd put his hat on his head and say:
"There's the bell! It's time to go."
It's time to study now, you know.
Tomorrow I'll finish the hat trick show."

SQUIRREL NAMED EARL

A squirrel named Earl,
He liked to twirl
His tail throughout the day.

He pestered the birds,
And snuck off with their food,
And his tail still twirled away.

He hopped to the birdbath
And took a small drink.
His tail kept twirling still.

He played in the garden
And jumped on the fence
And chased his brother, Will.

But one day, Earl, he lost his twirl—
And he was feeling ill.

"Oh my goodness gracious, Earl,
What's wrong?" asked brother Will.

"My tail's too tired to twirl," said Earl.
"I just don't feel so well."

"I'm just too tired to climb a tree,"
said Earl the squirrel as he fell.

He fell right down upon the ground
Into a deep, deep sleep.

His brother Will watched over him
And did not make a squeak.

Earl slept and slept and then awoke.
"Oh I hope I hope my tail still twirls!"
Said Earl and held it high.
He hopped around from tree to tree
And then began to fly!

"I'm back. I'm back,"
Said Earl aloud,
"I'm really, really me!"

My tail still twirls.
See how it whirls!
Yippee! Yippee! Yippeeeeeeee!"

A TURTLE NAMED SHELLY

A turtle named Shelly liked to play.
He crawled on his belly in the grass all day.

When he came inside, his mother said "Shelly!
You need a bath. You're very smelly!"

"I'm not *that* smelly," said Shelly.
"Yes you are, Shelly,
You're *awfully* smelly."

So Shelly took a bath.
He played with his boats
And scrubbed with soap.
Then Shelly wasn't smelly.

The next day, Shelly went out to play.
He crawled on his belly in the mud all day.

When he came inside, his mother said, "Shelly!
You need a bath. You're very smelly!"

"I'm not *that* smelly," said Shelly.
"Yes you are, Shelly,
You're *terribly* smelly."

So Shelly took a bath.
He played with his ducks
And poured water from cups.
Then Shelly wasn't smelly.

The next day, Shelly went out to play.
He crawled on his belly in the slime all day.

When he came inside, his mother said, "Shelly!
You need a bath. You're very smelly!"

"I'm not *that* smelly," said Shelly.
"Yes you are, my little Shelly,
You're *awfully, terribly, horribly* smelly."

So Shelly took a bath.
He played with his blocks
And he played with his ducks
And his dinosaurs
And his plastic cups.
Then Shelly wasn't smelly.

And from then on, Shelly, who liked to play,
Remembered to take a bath every day.

A LITTLE GIRL NAMED KEMPIE PEARL

A little girl named Kempie Pearl
Was a very "no, no" girl.

"Time to get up," said Mommy.
"No, no," said Kempie Pearl.
"Time for breakfast," said Daddy.
"No, no," said Kempie Pearl.
"Let's go for a walk now, honey."
"No, later," said Kempie Pearl,
Shaking her head and her curls.

Kempie, Kempie, Kempie Pearl
Was a little "no, no" girl.

"Time for lunch," said Mommy.
"No, no," said Kempie Pearl.
"Let's take a nap now, Sweetie."
"No, no," said Kempie Pearl.
"It's time to pick up," said Daddy.
"No, later," said Kempie Pearl,
Shaking her head and her curls.

Kempie, Kempie, Kempie Pearl
Was a little "no, no" girl.

"Here's supper for you, darling."
"No, no," said Kempie Pearl.
"And now a book and into bed."
"No, no," said Kempie Pearl.
"Good night. We love you," said Mommy.
"Do you love us too?"

And Kempie Pearl said: "Yes I do!
I love you and Daddy, too!"

Kempie, Kempie, Kempie Pearl
The very "no, no" little girl
Knew how to say "yes"
When it really mattered.

Made in the USA
Middletown, DE
28 March 2017